LOCAL RED BOOKS

CW00350151

PENZANCE
ST. IVES

HAYLE · NEWLYN · ST. JUST

LEGEND

══════	Minor Road
▨▨▨▨	Pedestrianized / Restricted Access
══════	Track
- - - - -	Footpath
⌇	Stream
∿∿∿	River
Lock	Canal
━━■━━	Railway / Station
●	Post Office
P	Car Park
C	Public Convenience
+	Place of Worship
→	One-way Street
i	Tourist Information Centre
8	Adjoining Pages
	Area Depicting Enlarged Centre
	General Buildings (Centre only)
	Woodland
	Recreation Ground
	Cemetery

CONTENTS

Page Layout & Road Map   **2**
3 Miles to 1 Inch

St. Ives Enlarged Centre   **7**
8 Inches to 1 Mile

Street Maps   **3-12**
4 Inches to 1 Mile

Index to Streets   **13**

Redbooks showing the way

Every effort has been made to verify the accuracy of information in this book but the publishers cannot accept responsibility for expense or loss caused by an error or omission.

Information that will be of assistance to the user of the maps will be welcomed.

The representation on these maps of a road, track or path is no evidence of the existence of a right of way.

Street plans prepared and published by ESTATE PUBLICATIONS, Bridewell House, TENTERDEN, KENT. The Publishers acknowledge the co-operation of the local authorities of towns represented in this atlas.

Ordnance Survey This product includes mapping data licensed from Ordnance Survey® with the permission of the Controller of Her Majesty's Stationery Office.

© Crown Copyright   All rights reserved
© Estate Publications 564-04   ISBN 1 84192 325 7   Licence number 100019031

www.ESTATE-PUBLICATIONS.co.uk

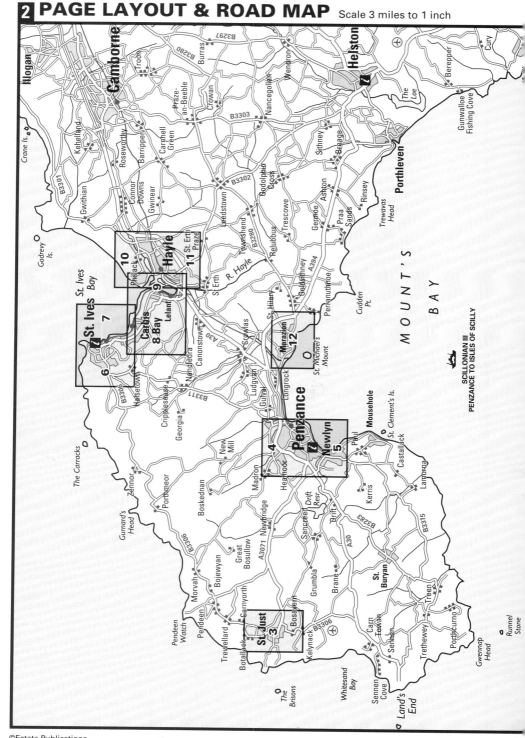

©Estate Publications

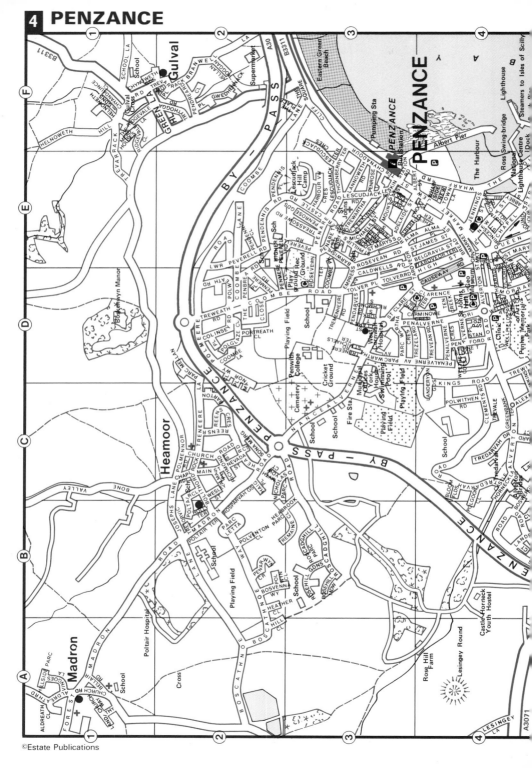

4 PENZANCE

©Estate Publications

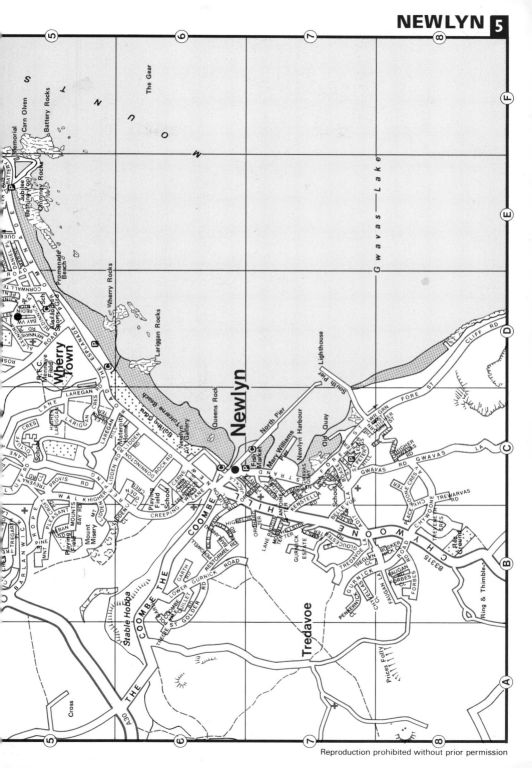

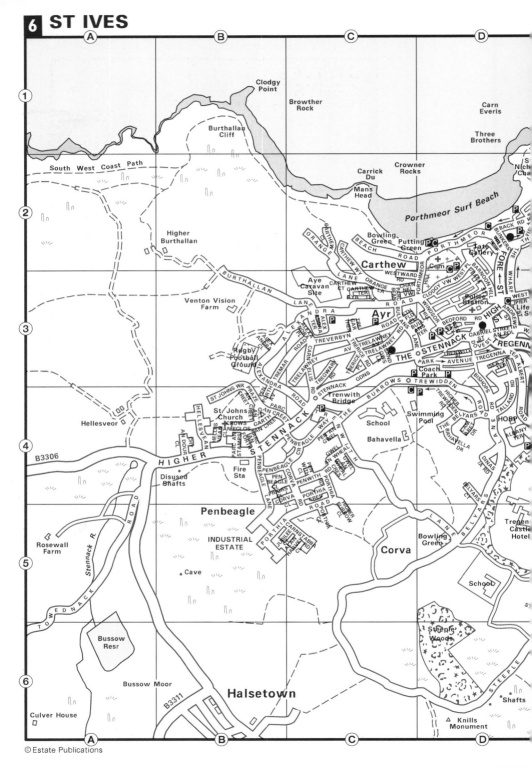

Clodgy Point

Browther Rock

Carn Everis

Three Brothers

Burthallan Cliff

South West Coast Path

Carrick Du

Crowner Rocks

Mans Head

Higher Burthallan

Porthmeor Surf Beach

Bowling Green

Putting Green

Carthew

Tate Gallery

Westward

BURTHALLAN LANE

Aye Caravan Site

Venton Vision Farm

Cem

Police Station

Ayr

Rugby Football Ground

Hellesveor

TREVERBYN

TRELAWNEY

THE STENNACK

Coach Park

Bedford

GABRIEL STREET

REGENNA

St Johns Church

Trenwith Bridge

BURROWS

TREWIDDEN

School

Swimming Pool

HIGHER STENNACK

Bahavella

Fire Sta

B3306

Disused Shafts

Penbeagle

PENWITH

PORTHIA

Corva

Tregen Castle Hotel

Rosewall Farm

Stennack R.

INDUSTRIAL ESTATE

Cave

Bowling Green

School

TOWEDNACK

Steeple Woods

Bussow Resr

Bussow Moor

B3311

Halsetown

STEEPLE

Shafts

Culver House

Knills Monument

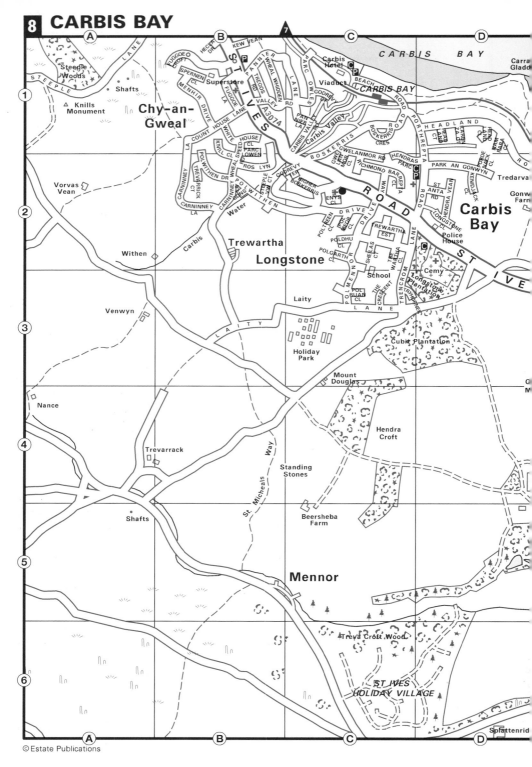

A **B** **C** **D**

Steeple Woods

Shafts

1 Knills Monument

Chy-an-Gweal

Vorvas Vean

2 Carbis

Withen

Trewartha Longstone

Venwyn

3 Holiday Park

Laity

Nance

4 Trevarrack

Standing Stones

Shafts

Beersheba Farm

5 **Mennor**

6 Treva Croft Wood

ST IVES HOLIDAY VILLAGE

Spattenrid

CARBIS BAY

Carbis Hotel

Viaduct

CARBIS BAY

Carra Gladd

Superstore

HEADLAND

BOSKERRIS CRES

GWELANMOR RD

RICHMOND

HENDRAS PARC

Tredarva

Park an Gonwyn

Gonw Farm

Carbis Bay

Police House

Cemy

Longstone Plantation

School

Cubic Plantation

Mount Douglas

Hendra Croft

St. Micheals Way

© Estate Publications

E F G H

1

Black Cliff

The Towans

Porth Kidney Sands

2

Hayle Towans

Riviere Chalet Camp

Riviere Towans

South West Coast Path

Links Hotel

Lelant Towans

Golf Course

Club Ho

North Quay 3

Harbour

noweth

CHURCH ROAD

East Quay

Cemy St Uny's Church

Manor House

10

PRAED PL

CHURCH CL

GREEN LANE

FAIRFIELD CL

Works

BREWERY HILL

RIVERSIDE

South Quay 4

LELANT MDWS

CHURCH ROAD

THE SALTINGS

CARNSEW MEADOW

TYRINGHAM ROAD

STATION HILL

LELANT

B3301

Lelant

VICARAGE LA

PLANTATION LA

CARNSEW ROAD

ABBEY MDWS

FORE STREET

ESTUARY VW

ST UNY CL

THE SALTINGS

RIVER HAYLE

revethoe Barton

BRUSH END

Elm Farm

TREND BEATH CL

Rec Grd

St Michaels Hospital

revethoe

ABBEY HILL

THE SALTINGS

Downes R C Convent 5

P

LELANT SALTINGS

Bird Garden

CHENHALLS ROAD

TRELISSICK RD

ALBERTUS GDNS

Leisure Park

Park & Ride

Griggs Quay

ROSCADWEN RD

ALBERTUS RD

MEADOWSIDE CLOSE

TRELISSICK RD

BOWNDER DOWN 6

MILL HILL

NUT LANE

A3074

GRIGGS HILL

THE CAUSEWAY

WATER LANE

A30

HAYLE BY-PASS A30

E F G H

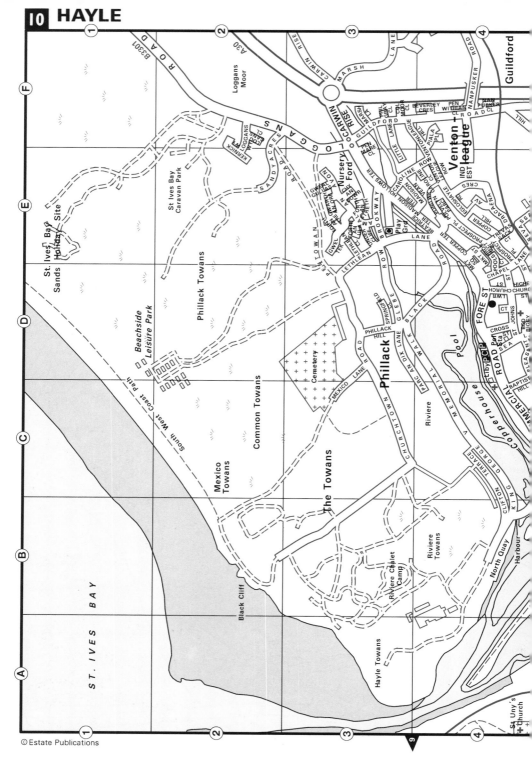

ST. IVES BAY

Guildford

Loggans Moor

Venton League

Phillack

Phillack Towans

St Ives Bay Caravan Park

St. Ives Bay Holiday Site

Sands

Beachside Leisure Park

Common Towans

Mexico Towans

The Towans

Black Cliff

South West Coast Path

Cemetery

Riviere

Riviere Towans

Riviere Chalet Camp

Hayle Towans

North Quay

Harbour

St Uny's church

Copperhouse Pool

Nursery Ford

Play Park

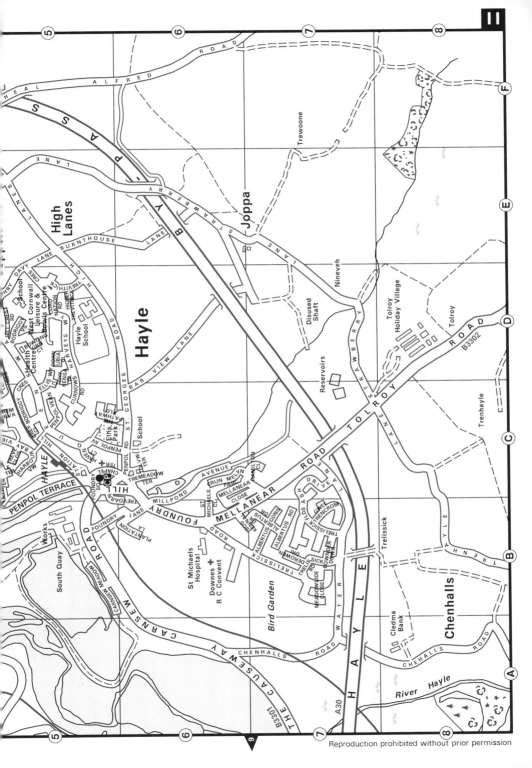

5 6 7 8

F

E

D

C

B

A

HEAL ALFRED ROAD

BYPASS

LANE

High
Lanes

Trewoone

Joppa

STRAWBERRY LANE

BURNTHOUSE LANE

Nineveh

HIGH LANES

HENRY DAVY CRES

School

West Cornwall
Leisure &
Baths Centre

Hayle
School

TREVITHICK RD

Hayle

Disused
Shaft

Tolroy
Holiday Village

Tolroy

ROAD

B3302

ST GEORGES ROAD

BAR VIEW LANE

Reservoirs

Trenhayle

TOLROY ROAD

STRAWBERRY LANE

PENPOL TER

Tremeadow
TER

AVENUE

BRUN MELYN

MELLANEAR
CLOSE

MELLANEAR ROAD

LANE

MILLPOND

ST MICHAELS
CL

ROAD

DRIVE

PENWITH RD

CRENCROM

Trelissick

HAYLE

TRENHAYLE LANE

PENPOL TERRACE

HAYLE STATION

FOUNDRY

CHAPEL
HILL

FOUNDRY HILL

TREVOARN

PLANTATION LANE

FOUNDRY LANE

FOUNDRY ROAD

St Michaels
Hospital

Downes
R C Convent

Bird Garden

TRELISSICK RD

ALBERTUS RD

ALBERTUS DM

FLDS ASH
DROWDER
DOWAH
SICKWIDER
DOWNER CLOSE
MEADOWSIDE
CLOSE

WATER

Chenhalls

Cledna
Bank

Works

South Quay

CARNSEW ROAD

CRANSWIN MEADOW

THE CAUSEWAY

CHENHALLS

CHENHALLS ROAD

ROAD

A30

B3301

River Hayle

5 6 7 8

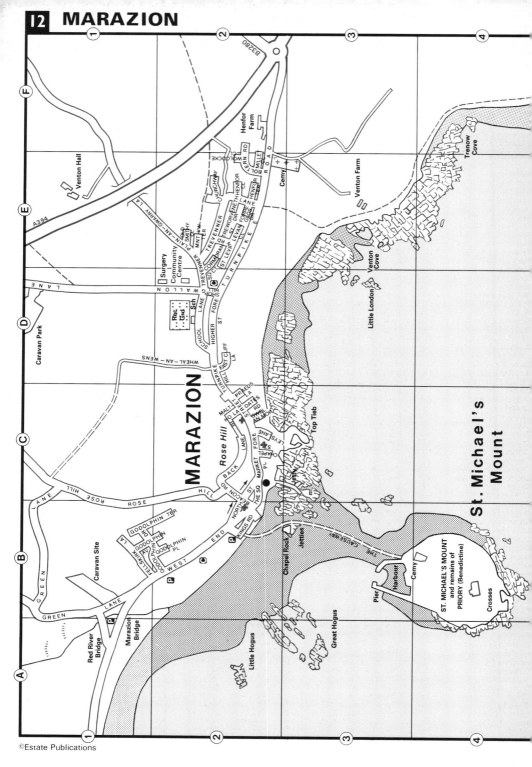

MARAZION

St. Michael's Mount

ST. MICHAEL'S MOUNT
and remains of
PRIORY (Benedictine)

Crosses

Cemy

Harbour

Pier

Chapel Rock

Jetties

THE CAUSEWAY

Little Hogus

Great Hogus

Top Tieb

Little London

Venton Cove

Trenow Cove

Venton Farm

Henfor Farm

Venton Hall

Caravan Park

Caravan Site

Red River Bridge

Marazion Bridge

GREEN LANE

ROSE HILL LANE

ROSE HILL

Rose Hill

WHEAL-AN-WENS

SCHOOL LANE

HIGHER ST

Rec. Grid

Sch

Surgery

Community Centre

PLAIN-AN-QUARRY LA

CHURCHWAY

A394

B3280

Cemy

WOLDCOCKE ROAD

BOLT TERN RD

HENFOR RD

MILLET

TREVENNER LANE

TREWORK CL

GLEBE

ST LEVAN

DINNETH

FORE ST

TURNPIKE

SMITHY

MNT VW

TREVENNER

TREVENNEN

SO CORNHILL

WALLON

TURNPIKE HILL

EAST CLIFF LA

MALT HO LANE

LEVANT RD

PARC

THE SQ

MARKET PL

CHAPEL

FORE ST

NORTH RD

KINGS RD

WEST END

GODOLPHIN PL

GODOLPHIN TER

FELLSHAM LA

BACK LANE

ST OATS

SWEL

ALMORE

LEYS LANE

LANE

Priory

A - Z INDEX TO STREETS
with Postcodes

he Index includes some
ames for which there is
nsufficient space on the maps.
hese names are indicated by
n * and are followed by the
earest adjoining thoroughfare.

HAYLE

Albertus Dri TR27	11 B7
Albertus Gdns TR27	11 B7
Albertus Rd TR27	11 B7
Amal An Avon TR27	10 E3
Ash Dri TR27	11 C7
Baptist Hill TR27	10 C4
Bar View La TR27	11 C6
Bay View Ter TR27	11 C5
Beatrice Ter TR27	10 E4
Beverley Cres TR27	10 F4
Black Rd TR27	10 D3
Bodriggy Ct TR27	10 D4
Bodriggy Cres TR27	11 C5
Bodriggy St TR27	10 D4
Bodriggy Villas TR27	11 D5
Boskennel Dri TR27	11 B7
Bowling Grn Ct TR27	11 D5
Bownder Dowr TR27	11 B7
Brookway TR27	10 E3
Burnthouse La TR27	11 E5
Carnsew Mdws TR27	11 B5
Carnsew Rd TR27	11 A6
Caroline Clo TR27	10 E4
Caroline Row TR27	10 E3
Carwin Rise TR27	10 F3
Chapel Hill TR27	10 C4
Chapel La TR27	10 D4
Chapel Ter TR27	11 C5
Chenhalls Rd TR27	11 A7
Churchtown Rd TR27	10 C3
Chy An Dowr TR27	10 E3
Chy Kensa Clo TR27	11 D5
Clifton Ter TR27	10 C4
Col-Moor Clo TR27	10 F3
Commercial Rd TR27	10 C4
Copper Hill TR27	10 E4
Copper Ter TR27	10 E4
Cornubia Clo TR27	11 D5
Coronation Rd TR27	11 D5
Crescent Clo TR27	11 C5
Cross St TR27	10 D4
Crun Melyn Parc TR27	11 C6
Curnows Rd TR27	11 C5
Derowen Dri TR27	11 B7
Dracaena Av TR27	10 E4
Dracaena Cres TR27	10 E4
East Ter TR27	11 C5
Egloshayle Rd TR27	10 E4
Ellis Clo TR27	11 C5
Ellis Way TR27	11 C5
Fore St TR27	10 D4
Forth An Streth TR27	10 E3
Forth An Tre TR27	10 E3
Forth An Ula TR27	10 E3
Foundry Hill TR27	11 B6
Foundry La TR27	11 B5
Foundry Sq TR27	11 C5
Glebe Row TR27	10 D3
Guildford Rd TR27	10 F3
Gwarth An Ore TR27	10 E3
Gweal Gollas TR27	10 E3
Gwel Tek TR27	10 E3
Gwel Trencrom TR27	11 B7
Hamilton Clo TR27	11 C7
Harbour View TR27	11 C5

Harveys Way TR27	11 D5
Haven Ct TR27	11 C5
Hayle By-Pass TR27	11 A7
Hayle Ter TR27	11 B5
High Lanes TR27	11 D5
Higher Church St TR27	10 D4
Higher Trevithick TR27	11 D5
Hill Crest Rd TR27	11 D5
Hollows Ter TR27	11 D5
Humphry Davy La TR27	11 D5
Kernick Way TR27	10 F2
King George V	
Memorial Wk TR27	10 C4
Lethlean Clo TR27	10 E3
Lethlean La TR27	10 E3
Little La TR27	10 F3
Loggans Clo TR27	10 F2
Loggans Rd TR27	10 F3
Loggans Way TR27	10 F2
Lower Church St TR27	10 D4
Madison Ter TR27	10 E3
Madison Vean TR27	10 E4
Market Sq TR27	10 D4
Market St TR27	10 E4
Marsh La TR27	10 F3
Meadowside Clo TR27	11 B7
Mellanear Clo TR27	11 C6
Mellanear Rd TR27	11 B6
Mexico La TR17	10 D3
Millpond Av TR27	11 B6
Mount Pleasant TR27	10 C4
Mount Pleasant Gdns	
TR27	11 C5
Nanpusker Clo TR27	10 F4
Nanpusker Rd TR27	10 F4
North Quay TR27	10 B4
Parc An Dix La TR27	10 D3
Penmare Clo TR27	10 E3
Penpol Av TR27	11 C5
Penpol Rd TR27	11 C6
Penpol Ter TR27	11 B5
Penpol Vean TR27	11 C5
Pentowan Rd TR27	10 E3
Penwithian Clo TR27	11 C5
Philgray Clo TR27	10 F3
Phillack Hill TR27	10 D3
Piala Pl TR27	10 F4
Plantation La TR27	11 B6
Polvelyn Parc TR27	11 C5
Pond Walk TR27	10 E4
Pools Ct TR27	10 E4
Prospect Pl TR27	10 E3
Queensway TR27	11 C5
St Georges Rd TR27	11 C6
St Johns Ct TR27	10 D4
St Johns St TR27	10 D4
St Michaels Clo TR27	11 B6
Sandyacres TR27	10 F2
Sea La TR27	10 D4
Springfield Clo TR27	10 D3
Station Hill TR27	11 C5
Strawberry La TR27	11 C7
The Causeway TR27	11 A7
The Pathway Flds TR27	11 C5
Tolroy Rd TR27	11 C7
Tolview Ter TR27	11 C6
Trelawney Pl TR27	11 D5
Trelawney Way TR27	10 D4
Trelissick Flds TR27	11 B7
Trelissick Rd TR27	11 B7
Tremeadow Ter TR27	11 C6
Tremorva TR27	11 C5
Trenhayle La TR27	11 B8
Trevassack Ct TR27	10 E4
Trevassack Hill TR27	10 E4
Treveglos TR27	11 C5

Trevithick Cres TR27	11 D5
Trevoarn TR27	11 B6
Undercliff TR27	10 E3
Ventonleague Hill TR27	10 E4
Ventonleague Row TR27	10 E4
Viaduct Hill TR27	11 E5
Water La TR27	11 A7
West Ter TR27	11 C5
Wheal Alfred Rd TR27	10 F4

MARAZION

Back La TR17	12 C2
Beacon Rd TR17	12 C2
Boltern Rd TR17	12 C2
Chapel St TR17	12 C2
Churchway TR17	12 E2
Cormoran Ct TR17	12 E2
East Cliff La TR17	12 D2
Feliskirk La TR17	12 B1
Fore St TR17	12 C2
Forreglos Dri TR17	12 E2
Godolphin Av TR17	12 B1
Godolphin Dri TR17	12 B2
Godolphin Pl TR17	12 B2
Godolphin Ter TR17	12 B1
Green La TR17	12 B1
Gwallon La TR17	12 D2
Gwel An Mor TR17	12 C2
Henfor Clo TR17	12 E2
Henfor Ter TR17	12 E2
Higher Fore St TR17	12 D2
Kings Rd TR17	12 B2
Leys La TR17	12 C2
Malthouse La TR17	12 C2
Market Pl TR17	12 C2
Millet Clo TR17	12 E2
Mount View Ter TR17	12 E2
North St TR17	12 C2
Oates Rd TR17	12 C2
Old Smithy Clo TR17	12 E1
Plain-An-Gwarry La	
TR17	12 E2
Praeds La TR17	12 C2
Rose Hill TR17	12 C1
St Levan Clo TR17	12 E2
St Levan Rd TR17	12 E2
School La TR17	12 D2
Shop Hill TR17	12 D2
The Causeway TR17	12 B3
The Square TR17	12 C2
Trevenner La TR17	12 E2
Trevenner Sq TR17	12 D2
Treworvenneth Dri TR17	12 E2
Turnpike Hill TR17	12 C2
Turnpike Rd TR17	12 D2
West End TR17	12 B2
Wheal-An-Wens TR17	12 D2
Woolcocke Clo TR17	12 E2

PENZANCE

Abbey St TR18	4 E4
Adelaide St TR18	4 E3
Adit La TR18	5 B7
Albert St TR18	4 E3
Albert Ter TR18	4 E3
Aldreath Clo TR20	4 A1
Aldreath Rd TR20	4 A1
Alexandra Gdns TR18	5 C5
Alexandra Pl TR18	5 D5
Alexandra Rd TR18	4 C4

Alexandra Ter TR18	5 C5
Alma Pl,	
Heamoor TR18	4 C2
Alma Pl,	
Penzance TR18	4 E4
Alma Ter TR18	4 E3
Alverne Bldgs TR18	4 D4
Alverton Rd TR18	4 C4
Alverton St TR18	4 D4
Antoine Ter TR18	5 B7
Barbican La TR18	5 E5
Barlandhu TR18	5 B6
Barlanwick TR18	5 B5
Barton Clo TR18	4 C2
Barwis Hill TR18	4 E3
Battery Rd TR18	5 E5
Bay View Ter TR18	5 D5
Beachfield St*,	
The Esplanade TR18	5 D5
Belgravia St TR18	4 E4
Bellair Rd TR20	4 A1
Bellevue TR18	5 B7
Bloomfields TR18	4 C4
Boase St TR18	5 C7
Bolitho Rd TR18	4 C2
Bon Cot Rd TR18	5 B6
Bone Valley TR18	4 C1
Boscathnoe La TR18	4 A2
Boscathnoe Way TR18	4 A2
Boskernick Clo TR18	5 B8
Bosvenna Way TR18	4 B2
Boswergy TR18	4 B4
Bowjey Hill TR18	5 C8
Bowjey Ter TR18	5 C8
Branwell La TR18	4 F2
Bread St TR18	4 E4
Caldwells Rd TR18	4 D3
Cardinnis Rd TR18	5 B5
Carminowe Cres TR18	4 D4
Carne Rd TR18	5 C6
Castle Horneck La TR18	4 C4
Castle Rd TR18	4 E3
Causewayhead TR18	4 D4
Chapel Rd TR18	4 C2
Chapel St,	
Newlyn TR18	5 C7
Chapel St,	
Penzance TR18	4 E4
Charles St TR18	5 C6
Cherry Gdns TR18	4 E4
Church Rd,	
Heamoor TR18	4 C2
Church Rd,	
Madron TR20	4 A1
Church St TR18	5 C7
Churchway TR20	4 A1
Chyandaunce Clo TR18	4 F1
Chyandour Cliff TR18	4 E3
Chynoweth Gdns TR18	4 F1
Chyvellas Clo TR18	5 B7
Chywoone Av TR18	5 B8
Chywoone Cres TR18	5 C8
Chywoone Hill TR18	5 B8
Chywoone Pl TR18	5 B8
Chywoone Ter TR18	5 C8
Clarence St TR18	4 D4
Clarence Ter TR18	4 D4
Clements Rd TR18	4 C4
Cliff Rd TR18	5 D8
Clifton Hill TR18	5 C6
Coinage Hall St TR18	5 E5
Colinsey Pl TR18	4 D2
Colinsey Rd TR18	4 D2
Coombe La TR18	4 D2
Coombe Park TR18	4 D3
Coombe Rd TR18	4 D2

Street	Ref		Street	Ref		Street	Ref		Street	Ref
Coombe Vale TR18	5 B6		Leskinnick Pl TR18	4 E3		Polgarth TR18	5 B6		Tolver Rd TR18	4 D
Cornwall Ter TR18	5 D5		Leskinnick St TR18	4 E3		Polglaze Clo TR18	4 D2		Treassowe Rd TR18	4 E
Coulsons Pl TR18	5 E5		Leskinnick Ter TR18	4 E3		Polgoon Clo TR18	4 C4		Treban Rd TR18	5 B
Coulsons Ter TR18	5 E5		Lidden Clo TR18	5 B6		Polmeere Rd TR18	4 D2		Tredarvah Dri TR18	4 C
Creeping La TR18	5 B6		Lidden Cres TR18	5 C6		Polmennor Rd TR18	4 C2		Tredarvah Rd TR18	4 C
Croft Rd TR18	5 B5		Lidden Rd TR18	5 C6		Poltair Clo TR18	4 B2		Tredavoe La TR18	5 B
Cross St TR18	4 E3		Love La TR18	5 C5		Poltair Ter TR18	4 B2		Tregarth Pl TR18	5 E
Custom House La TR18	4 E4		Lower Green St TR18	5 C7		Polventon Clo TR18	4 B2		Tregie TR18	5 A
Daniel Pl TR18	5 E5		Lower Gurnick Rd TR18	5 B6		Polweath Rd TR18	4 D2		Treglyn Clo TR18	5 E
Dock La TR18	4 E4		Lower Peverell Rd TR18	4 E2		Polwithen Rd TR18	4 C4		Tregoddick Clo TR20	4 A
Dominic St TR18	4 E3		Madron Rd TR20	4 A1		Polwyn Clo TR18	4 B2		Tremaine Clo TR18	4 B
Donnington Rd TR18	5 C6		Main St TR18	4 C2		Princes St TR18	4 E4		Tremenheere Rd TR18	4 D
East Ter TR18	4 E3		Manor Clo TR18	4 D2		Promenade TR18	5 D5		Treneere La TR18	4 C
Eden Gdns TR18	5 C7		Manor Pl TR18	4 D2		Provis Rd TR18	5 C5		Treneere Rd TR18	4 D
Elm Way TR18	5 C7		Manor Way TR18	4 D2		Quay St TR18	4 E4		Treneglos Ter TR18	5 C
Elms Close Ter TR18	5 B7		Marine Ter TR18	5 E5		Queen St TR18	4 E4		Trenoweth Cres TR18	5 B
Empress Av TR18	4 D3		Market Jew St TR18	4 E4		Quillet Rd TR18	5 B6		Trenoweth Rd TR18	5 B
Faugan La TR18	5 B8		Market Pl TR18	4 E4		Redinnick Gdns TR18	5 D5		Trerew Rd TR18	5 B
Faugan Rd TR18	5 B8		Mennaye Rd TR18	5 D5		Redinnick Pl TR18	5 D5		Tretorvic Ter TR18	4 B
Forbes Clo TR18	5 B8		Morrab Pl TR18	4 D4		Redinnick Ter TR18	5 D5		Trevale TR18	4 C
Forbes Rd TR18	5 B8		Morrab Rd TR18	4 D4		Reens Cres TR18	4 C2		Trevarrack Pl TR18	4 F
Fore St,			Morrab Ter TR18	4 D4		Reens Rd TR18	4 C2		Trevarrack Rd TR18	4 E
Madron TR20	4 A1		Mount Lidden TR18	5 B5		Regent Sq TR18	4 E4		Trevean Rd TR18	4 D
Fore St,			Mount Pleasant TR18	5 B5		Regent Ter TR18	5 E5		Trevena Clo TR18	5 C
Newlyn TR18	5 C7		Mount St TR18	4 E3		Restormel Rd TR18	5 B6		Trevena Rd TR18	5 C
Foundry La TR18	5 C7		Mount View Ter TR18	5 B7		Richmond St TR18	4 D3		Treveneth Cres TR18	5 B
Fradgan Pl TR18	5 C7		Mounts Bay Rd TR18	5 B5		Richmond St,			Trewartha Ter TR18	4 E
Garth Rd TR18	5 B6		Mythyow Ct TR18	4 C2		Heamoor TR18	4 C2		Trewarvas Rd TR18	5 C
Gloucester Pl TR18	5 B7		Nancealverne TR18	4 C3		Ridgevale Clo TR18	4 F1		Trewarveneth St TR18	5 C
Gloucester Rd TR18	5 B7		Nevada St TR18	4 C2		Ridgevale La TR18	4 F1		Treweath Rd TR18	4 D
Green Lane Hill TR18	4 F2		New Rd TR18	5 C6		Rock Rd TR18	5 C6		Trewithen Rd TR18	4 D
Green Market TR18	4 E4		New St TR18	4 E4		Rock Ter TR18	4 C2		Trezela Rd TR18	4 D
Green St Gdns TR18	5 E5		Newtown La TR18	4 E4		Rope Walk TR18	5 B5		Trythogga Rd TR18	4 F
Greenbank Ter TR18	4 C4		Nicholas Parc TR18	4 C2		Roscadghill Parc TR18	4 B3		Under Chapel TR18	5 E
Gurnick Est TR18	5 B7		North Corner TR18	5 C7		Roscadghill Rd TR18	4 B3		Union St TR18	4 E
Gurnick Rd TR18	5 B7		North Parade TR18	4 D4		Rosehill Gdns TR18	4 B3		Vellan Hoggan TR18	4 F
Gwavas La TR18	5 C8		Old Paul Hill TR18	5 B6		Rosehill Mdws TR18	4 B3		Victoria Pl TR18	4 D
Gwavas Quay TR18	5 C7		Orchard Ct TR18	4 C4		Roseparvah Gdns TR18	4 B2		Victoria Sq TR18	4 E
Gwavas Rd TR18	5 C7		Orchard Pl TR18	5 C7		Rosevale TR18	5 D5		Vingoes La TR18	4 A
Gwavas St TR18	4 E3		Orchard Ter TR18	5 B7		Rosevean Rd TR18	4 E3		Voundervour La TR18	4 E
Gwedhennack TR18	4 F2		Parade Pl TR18	4 E4		Rosevean Ter TR18	4 D3		Weeths Cotts TR18	4 D
Haig Pl TR18	4 C2		Parade TR18	4 E4		St Clare St TR18	4 D3		Wellfields TR18	4 D
Harbour Vw Cres TR18	4 E3		Parc Letta TR18	4 B2		St Clare Ter TR18	4 D3		Wellington Ter TR18	4 D
Hawkins Rd TR18	4 D4		Parc Mellan TR18	4 D2		St Francis St*,			Wesley St TR18	4 C
Hea Ct TR18	4 C2		Parc Wartha Av TR18	4 D3		Barwis Hill TR18	4 E3		West Ter TR18	5 C
Hea Rd TR18	4 C2		Parc Wartha Cres TR18	4 D3		St Golder Rd TR18	5 B6		Wharf Rd TR18	4 E
Heabrook Parc TR18	4 B3		Park Corner TR18	4 D4		St Henry St TR18	4 E3		Wharfside TR18	4 E
Heather Clo TR18	4 B2		Park Rd TR18	5 B7		St James St TR18	4 E4		Wharfside Village*,	
Helnoweth Gdns TR18	4 F1		Park Ter TR18	5 B7		St Johns Ter TR18	4 E3		Wharfside TR18	4 E
Helnoweth Hill TR18	4 F1		Penalverne Av TR18	4 D4		St Marys St TR18	4 E3		Wherry Town*,	
High St TR18	4 D4		Penalverne Cres TR18	4 D4		St Marys Ter TR18	4 E4		The Esplanade TR18	5 D
Higher Green St TR18	5 C8		Penalverne Dri TR18	4 D4		St Michaels St TR18	4 E3		Windsor Ter TR18	4 D
Higher Gwavas Rd TR18	5 C8		Penalverne Pl TR18	4 D4		St Michaels Ter TR18	4 D3		Wood St TR18	4 E
Higher Larrigan TR18	5 C5		Penare Rd TR18	4 E3		St Peters Hill TR18	5 C7		York St TR18	4 D
Higher Lidden Rd TR18	5 C5		Penare Ter TR18	4 E3		St Peters Pl TR18	5 C7			
Higher Peverell Rd TR18	4 E2		Penarwyn Cres TR18	4 B2		St Phillip St TR18	4 E3			
Highfields TR18	5 B7		Penbrea Rd TR18	4 D2		St Warren St*,				
Hill Clo TR18	4 A2		Pendarves Rd TR18	4 D3		Barwis Hill TR18	4 E3			
Hillside Parc TR18	4 A1		Pendennis Clo TR18	4 E2		School La TR18	4 F1			

ST. IVES/ LELANT

Street	Ref
Hillside Ter TR18	4 A1
Holly Ter TR18	4 B2
Jack La TR18	5 C6
Jennings St TR18	4 E4
Josephs La TR18	4 B2
Kenstella Rd TR18	5 C7
Kings Rd TR18	4 D4
Landeryon Gdns TR18	4 C4
Landithy TR20	4 A1
Lane Reddin Ter TR18	5 B7
Lannoweth Rd TR18	4 E3
Lansdowne Clo TR18	4 B4
Lansdowne Ct TR18	4 B4
Lansdowne Pl TR18	5 B5
Lansdowne Rd TR18	4 B4
Laregan Hill TR18	5 C5
Laregan Rd TR18	5 C5
Larrigan Cres TR18	5 C5
Lescudjack Cres TR18	4 E3
Lescudjack Rd TR18	4 E3
Lescudjack Ter TR18	4 E3
Lesingey La TR18	4 A4

Street	Ref
Pendennis Pl TR18	4 E2
Pendennis Rd TR18	4 E2
Pendrea Clo TR18	4 F2
Pendrea Pl TR18	4 F2
Pendrea Rd TR18	4 F2
Pengwell TR18	5 B6
Penkernick Clo TR18	5 B7
Penlee Manor Dri TR18	5 D5
Penlee St TR18	4 E3
Penlee View Ter TR18	5 D5
Penmere Clo TR18	4 D2
Penmere Pl TR18	4 D2
Penmere Rd TR18	4 D2
Penpons Clo TR18	5 C5
Penrose Gdns TR18	4 E3
Penrose Ter TR18	4 E3
Pentreath Clo TR18	4 D2
Penwith St TR18	4 E3
Penzance By-Pass TR18	4 B4
Peverell Rd TR18	4 E3
Pine Rd TR18	5 B5

Street	Ref
Sona Merg TR18	4 C2
South Pl TR18	4 D4
Stanford Ter TR18	4 D4
Station Rd TR18	4 E3
Strand TR18	5 C7
Tarovoer Rd TR18	4 D3
Tarovoer Ter TR18	4 E4
Tencreek Av TR18	4 D4
The Close TR18	4 D2
The Coombe TR18	5 A6
The Esplanade TR18	5 D5
The Fradgan TR18	5 C7
The Green TR18	5 C7
The Mead Houses TR18	4 F1
The Place TR18	4 F3
The Quay TR18	4 E4
The Square TR18	4 F3
The Terrace TR18	4 E4
Thornberry Ter TR18	4 E3
Toltuff Cres TR18	5 C5
Toltuff Rd TR18	5 C5
Tolver Pl TR18	4 D3

Street	Ref
Abbey Hill TR26	9 F
Abbey Mdws TR26	9 F
Academy Pl TR26	7 J
Academy Ter TR27	7 J
Alan Harvey Clo TR26	6 C
Albany Ter TR26	6 D
Albert Rd TR26	6 D
Alexandra Clo TR26	6 B
Alexandra Pl TR26	6 C
Alexandra Rd TR26	6 B
Alexandra Ter TR26	6 C
Atlantic Ter TR26	7 J
Ayr La TR26	7 J
Ayr Ter TR26	6 C
Back Rd East TR26	7 K
Back Rd West TR26	6 D
Back St TR26	6 D
Bahavella Dri TR26	6 D
Baileys La TR26	7 K
Barnawoon TR27	7 J
Barnoon Hill TR26	6 D

14

arnoon Ter TR26 7 J7
arrepta Clo TR26 8 C2
each Rd,
Carbis Bay TR26 8 C1
each Rd, St Ives TR26 6 C2
edford Pl TR26 7 J8
edford Rd TR26 6 D3
ellair Ter TR26 7 J8
elyars Ct TR26 6 D4
elyars La TR26 6 D5
ethesda Hill TR26 7 K7
ethesda Pl TR26 7 K7
ishops Rd TR26 6 D3
oskerris Cres TR26 8 C1
oskerris Rd TR26 8 C1
owling Green Ter TR26 7 J8
rewery Hill TR26 9 G4
rush End TR26 9 F5
ullans La TR26 6 C3
ullans Ter TR26 6 D3
unkers Hill TR26 6 D2
urrow Rd TR26 7 K7
urthallan La TR26 6 B3
amaret Dri TR26 6 D4
arbis Valley Rd TR26 8 C1
arn Ellis Rd TR26 6 C3
arncrows St TR26 7 K7
arnglaze Pl TR26 7 K7
arninney La TR26 8 B2
arnstabba Rd TR26 6 C5
arrack Dhu Ter TR26 7 J8
arthew Clo TR26 6 C2
arthew Ct TR26 6 C3
arthew Ter TR26 6 C3
arthew Way TR26 6 C2
hannel View TR26 6 C3
hapel St TR26 7 J8
hurch Clo TR26 9 F4
hurch La TR26 9 F3
hurch Pl TR16 7 K7
hurch Pl TR26 9 F4
hy An Dour Clo TR26 6 B4
lodgy Vw TR26 6 D3
orva Clo TR26 6 C4
orva Rd TR26 6 C4
ount House La TR26 8 B1
ourt Cocking TR26 7 J8
rows-an-Eglos TR26 6 B4
inas la Rd TR26 6 D4
ove St TR26 6 D3
nys Clo TR26 8 C2
stuary View TR26 9 F5
airfield Clo TR26 9 G4
ish St TR26 6 D2
ore St, Lelant TR26 9 F5
ore St, St Ives TR26 6 D2
uggoe Croft TR26 7 E6
uggoe La TR26 8 B1
abriel St TR26 6 D3
arth An Creet TR26 6 B4
ill An Creet TR26 6 B4
odrevy Ct TR26 8 C1
odrevy Ter TR26 8 C2
reen La TR26 9 G3
riggis Hill TR27 9 F6
wel An Wheal TR26 6 C4
Gwel An Wheal Cres
TR26 6 C4
welanmor Clo TR26 8 C2
welanmor Rd TR26 8 C2
eadland Clo TR26 8 D1
eadland Ct TR26 8 D1

Headland Rd TR26 8 D1
Hecla Dri TR26 7 E6
Hellesvean TR26 6 B4
Hellesvean Clo TR26 6 B4
Hendra Vean TR26 8 D2
Hendras Parc TR26 8 C2
Hicks Ct TR26 7 J7
High St TR26 6 D3
Higher Burrow Clo TR26 6 C4
Higher Boskerris TR26 8 C2
Higher Stennack TR26 6 B4
Higher Tregenna Rd
TR26 7 E5
Higher Trewidden Rd
TR26 6 D4
Island Rd TR26 7 K7
Island Sq TR26 7 K7
Jubilee Ct TR26 6 B5
Karenza Ct TR26 8 D1
Kenidjack Clo TR26 8 D2
Kew Vean TR26 7 E6
Knill Clo TR26 8 B2
Laity La TR26 8 B3
Lelant Mdws TR26 9 F4
Longstone Clo TR26 8 D2
Manor Dri TR26 7 E5
Market Pl TR26 7 J8
Market Strand TR26 7 J8
Menhir Dri TR26 8 B1
Mill Hill TR26 9 E6
Mount Zion TR26 7 K7
Nampara Clo TR26 8 D1
Norway La TR26 7 K7
Norway Sq TR26 7 J7
Nut La TR26 9 F6
Orange La TR26 6 C3
Pannier La TR26 8 B1
Parc An Creet TR26 6 B4
Parc An Forth TR26 6 B4
Parc An Stamps TR26 6 B4
Park Bean TR26 6 C3
Parc Lowen TR26 8 B1
Parc Owles TR26 8 C1
Park An Gonwyn TR26 8 D2
Park Av TR26 6 D3
Pednolva Wk TR26 7 K8
Pen An Gwel TR26 6 C4
Pen Porth Av TR26 6 B4
Penbeagle Clo TR26 6 C4
Penbeagle Cres TR26 6 B4
Penbeagle La TR26 6 B4
Penbeagle Way TR26 6 C4
Penwith Clo TR26 6 C4
Penwith Rd TR26 6 C4
Poldhu Clo TR26 8 C2
Polgarth Clo TR26 8 C2
Polmennor Dri TR26 8 C3
Polmeor Clo TR26 8 C2
Polruan Clo TR26 8 C3
Poltreen Clo TR26 8 B2
Polwithen Dri TR26 8 B2
Polwithen Gdns TR26 8 B2
Pordenack Clo TR26 8 D2
Porthrepta Rd TR26 8 C1
Porthia Clo TR26 6 C5
Porthia Cres TR26 6 C4
Porthia Rd TR26 6 C4
Porthmeor TR26 6 D2
Porthmeor Hill TR26 6 D2
Porthmeor Rd TR26 7 K7
Porthmeor Sq TR26 7 J7
Praed Pl TR26 9 F3

Praze An Creet TR26 6 B4
Primrose Valley TR26 7 E4
Priors Clo TR26 6 B4
Richmond Pl TR26 8 J8
Richmond Way TR26 8 C2
Riverside TR26 9 G4
Ros Lyn TR26 8 B2
Rose La TR26 7 J7
St Andrews St TR26 6 D3
St Anta Rd TR26 8 D2
St Eia St TR26 7 K7
St Ives Rd TR26 7 E6
St Johns Wk TR26 6 B4
St Peters St TR26 7 K7
St Uny Clo TR26 9 F5
Salubrious Ter TR26 7 J7
Saltings Clo TR26 9 F5
Sandows La TR26 6 C3
Sea View Pl TR26 7 K7
Sea View Ter TR26 6 D3
Sheilas Ct TR26 8 C2
Skidden Hill TR26 7 K8
Smeatons Pier TR26 7 K7
Southfield Pl TR26 6 C3
Spernen Clo TR26 8 B1
Station Hill TR26 9 F4
Steeple Clo TR26 6 D5
Steeple La TR26 6 D6
Steeple View Ct TR26 6 D5
Stennack Gdns TR26 6 C3
Street An Garrow TR26 8 J8
Street An Pol TR26 6 D3
Talland Rd TR26 6 D4
Teetotal St TR26 7 K7
The Belyars TR26 6 D4
The Burrows TR26 6 C4
The Crescent TR26 8 C3
The Digey TR26 7 J7
The Meadow TR16 7 J7
The Rope Walk TR26 7 K7
The Saltings TR26 9 F5
The Stennack TR26 6 D3
The Terrace TR26 6 D3
The Warren TR26 6 D3
The Wharf TR26 6 D2
Towednack Rd TR26 6 A5
Tregarthen TR26 6 D3
Tregenna Hill TR26 6 D3
Tregenna Parc TR26 7 E5
Tregenna Pl TR26 7 J8
Tregenna Ter TR26 6 D3
Tregos Rd TR26 8 B1
Tregwary Rd TR26 6 D3
Trelawney Av TR26 6 C3
Trelawney Rd TR26 6 C3
Trelissick Rd TR27 9 H6
Treloyhan Clo TR26 7 E5
Treloyhan Pk Rd TR26 7 E5
Trelyon Av TR26 6 D4
Tremar Rd TR26 6 B3
Trencrom La TR26 8 C3
Trendreath Clo TR26 9 F5
Trenwith La TR26 6 C4
Trenwith Pl TR26 6 D3
Trerice Pl TR26 6 C3
Trerice Rd TR26 6 C3
Trevarrick Ct TR26 8 B2
Treverbyn Rd TR26 6 C3
Trewartha Clo TR26 8 C2
Trewartha Est TR26 8 C2
Trewidden Rd TR26 6 D3
Tryhornek TR26 8 C3

Tyringham Rd TR26 9 F4
Valley Rd TR26 8 B1
Venton Rd TR26 7 E5
Vicarage La TR26 9 F4
Victoria Pl TR26 7 K7
Victoria Rd TR26 7 K7
Virgin St TR26 7 J7
Wesley Pl TR26 6 D3
West Pier TR26 6 D3
West Pl TR26 6 D3
Westward Rd TR26 6 C3
Wheal Dream TR26 7 K7
Wheal Margery TR26 7 E6
Wheal Speed Rd TR26 8 B2
Wheal Venture Rd TR26 7 E6
Wheal Whidden TR26 8 B1
White House Clo TR26 8 B1
Wills La TR26 7 J8
Windsor Hill TR26 6 D3

ST. JUST

Bank Sq TR19 3 C3
Bethany Pl TR19 3 C4
Bosorne Clo TR19 3 A4
Bosorne Rd TR19 3 A4
Bosorne St TR19 3 A4
Bosorne Ter TR19 3 B4
Boswedden Rd TR19 3 A2
Cape Cornwall Rd TR19 3 A3
Cape Cornwall St TR19 3 B3
Carn Bosavern TR19 3 C5
Carn Bosavern Clo TR19 3 C5
Carrallack La TR19 3 B5
Carrallack Mews TR19 3 B5
Carrallack Ter TR19 3 B6
Chapel Rd TR19 3 B3
Chapel St TR19 3 B3
Church St TR19 3 C3
Fore St TR19 3 C4
Lafrowda Clo TR19 3 B4
Lafrowda Ter TR19 3 C4
Market Sq TR19 3 C3
Market St TR19 3 B4
Nancherrow Hill TR19 3 B2
Nancherrow Row TR19 3 C1
Nancherrow Ter TR19 3 B2
New Rd TR19 3 D2
No Go By Hill TR19 3 C1
North Row TR19 3 C3
Old Foundry Clo TR19 3 D1
Pednandrea TR19 3 A2
Penzance Rd TR19 3 C5
Pleasant Ter TR19 3 A4
Princess St TR19 3 A4
Queen St TR19 3 A4
Regent Ter TR19 3 A4
South Pl TR19 3 B5
South Pl Gdns TR19 3 B5
The Turnpike TR19 3 D2
Tregeseal Row TR19 3 D1
Tregeseal Ter TR19 3 D1
Venton East Hill TR19 3 D3
Venton East Sq TR19 3 C3
Victoria Row TR19 3 B4
Vounder Glaze TR19 3 B4
West Pl TR19 3 B4

ESTATE PUBLICATIONS

RED BOOKS

ALDERSHOT, CAMBERLEY
ALFRETON, BELPER, RIPLEY
ASHFORD, TENTERDEN
AYLESBURY, TRING
BANGOR, CAERNARFON
BARNSTAPLE, BIDEFORD
BASILDON, BILLERICAY
BASINGSTOKE, ANDOVER
BATH, BRADFORD-ON-AVON
BEDFORD
BIRMINGHAM, WOLVERHAMPTON, COVENTRY
BODMIN, WADEBRIDGE
BOURNEMOUTH, POOLE, CHRISTCHURCH
BRACKNELL
BRENTWOOD
BRIGHTON, LEWES, NEWHAVEN, SEAFORD
BRISTOL
BROMLEY (London Borough)
BURTON-UPON-TRENT, SWADLINCOTE
BURY ST. EDMUNDS
CAMBRIDGE
CARDIFF
CARLISLE
CHELMSFORD, BRAINTREE, MALDON, WITHAM
CHESTER
CHESTERFIELD
CHICHESTER, BOGNOR REGIS
CHIPPENHAM, CALNE
COLCHESTER, CLACTON
CORBY, KETTERING
COVENTRY
CRAWLEY & MID SUSSEX
CREWE
DERBY, HEANOR, CASTLE DONINGTON
EASTBOURNE, BEXHILL, SEAFORD, NEWHAVEN
EDINBURGH, MUSSELBURGH, PENICUIK
EXETER, EXMOUTH
FALKIRK, GRANGEMOUTH
FAREHAM, GOSPORT
FLINTSHIRE TOWNS
FOLKESTONE, DOVER, DEAL & ROMNEY MARSH
GLASGOW, & PAISLEY
GLOUCESTER, CHELTENHAM
GRAVESEND, DARTFORD
GRAYS, THURROCK
GREAT YARMOUTH, LOWESTOFT
GRIMSBY, CLEETHORPES
GUILDFORD, WOKING
HARLOW, BISHOPS STORTFORD
HARROGATE, KNARESBOROUGH
HASTINGS, BEXHILL, RYE
HEREFORD
HERTFORD, HODDESDON, WARE
HIGH WYCOMBE
HUNTINGDON, ST. NEOTS
IPSWICH, FELIXSTOWE
ISLE OF MAN
ISLE OF WIGHT TOWNS
KENDAL, WINDERMERE
KIDDERMINSTER
KINGSTON-UPON-HULL
LANCASTER, MORECAMBE
LEICESTER, LOUGHBOROUGH
LINCOLN
LLANDUDNO, COLWYN BAY
LUTON, DUNSTABLE
MACCLESFIELD
MAIDSTONE
MANSFIELD, MANSFIELD WOODHOUSE
MEDWAY, GILLINGHAM
MILTON KEYNES
NEW FOREST TOWNS
NEWBURY, THATCHAM
NEWPORT, CHEPSTOW
NEWQUAY
NEWTOWN, WELSHPOOL
NORTHAMPTON
NORTHWICH, WINSFORD
NORWICH
NOTTINGHAM, EASTWOOD, HUCKNALL, ILKESTON
NUNEATON, BEDWORTH
OXFORD, ABINGDON
PENZANCE, ST. IVES
PETERBOROUGH
PLYMOUTH, IVYBRIDGE, SALTASH, TORPOINT
PORTSMOUTH, HAVANT, WATERLOOVILLE
READING

REDDITCH, BROMSGROVE
REIGATE, BANSTEAD, LEATHERHEAD, DORKING
RHYL, PRESTATYN
RUGBY
ST. ALBANS, WELWYN, HATFIELD
ST. AUSTELL
SALISBURY, AMESBURY, WILTON
SCUNTHORPE
SEVENOAKS
SHREWSBURY
SITTINGBOURNE, FAVERSHAM, ISLE OF SHEPPEY
SLOUGH, MAIDENHEAD, WINDSOR
SOUTHAMPTON, EASTLEIGH
SOUTHEND-ON-SEA
STAFFORD
STEVENAGE, HITCHIN, LETCHWORTH
STIRLING
STOKE-ON-TRENT
STROUD, NAILSWORTH
SWANSEA, NEATH, PORT TALBOT
SWINDON, CHIPPENHAM, MARLBOROUGH
TAUNTON, BRIDGWATER
TELFORD
THANET, CANTERBURY, HERNE BAY, WHITSTABLE
TORBAY (Torquay, Paignton, Newton Abbot)
TRURO, FALMOUTH
TUNBRIDGE WELLS, TONBRIDGE, CROWBOROUGH
WARWICK, ROYAL LEAMINGTON SPA &
    STRATFORD UPON AVON
WATFORD, HEMEL HEMPSTEAD
WELLINGBOROUGH
WESTON-SUPER-MARE, CLEVEDON
WEYMOUTH, DORCHESTER
WINCHESTER, NEW ARLESFORD
WORCESTER, DROITWICH
WORTHING, LITTLEHAMPTON, ARUNDEL
WREXHAM
YORK

COUNTY RED BOOKS (Town Centre Maps)

BEDFORDSHIRE
BERKSHIRE
BUCKINGHAMSHIRE
CAMBRIDGESHIRE
CHESHIRE
CORNWALL
DERBYSHIRE
DEVON
DORSET
ESSEX
GLOUCESTERSHIRE
HAMPSHIRE
HEREFORDSHIRE
HERTFORDSHIRE
KENT
LEICESTERSHIRE & RUTLAND
LINCOLNSHIRE
NORFOLK
NORTHAMPTONSHIRE
NOTTINGHAMSHIRE
OXFORDSHIRE
SHROPSHIRE
SOMERSET
STAFFORDSHIRE
SUFFOLK
SURREY
SUSSEX (EAST)
SUSSEX (WEST)
WILTSHIRE
WORCESTERSHIRE

OTHER MAPS

KENT TO CORNWALL (1:460,000)
CHINA (1:6,000,000)
INDIA (1:3,750,000)
INDONESIA (1:4,000,000)
NEPAL (1,800,000)
SOUTH EAST ASIA (1:6,000,000)
THAILAND (1:1,600,000)

STREET PLANS

CARDIFF
EDINBURGH TOURIST PLAN
ST. ALBANS
WOLVERHAMPTON

OFFICIAL TOURIST & LEISURE MAPS

SOUTH EAST ENGLAND (1:200,000)
KENT & EAST SUSSEX (1:150,000)
SUSSEX & SURREY (1:150,000)
SUSSEX (1:50,000)
SOUTHERN ENGLAND (1:200,000)
ISLE OF WIGHT (1:50,000)
WESSEX (1:200,000)
DORSET (1:150,000)
DEVON & CORNWALL (1:200,000)
CORNWALL (1:180,000)
DEVON (1:200,000)
DARTMOOR & SOUTH DEVON COAST (1:100,000)
EXMOOR & NORTH DEVON COAST (1:100,000)
GREATER LONDON M25 (1:80,000)
EAST ANGLIA (1:200,000)
CHILTERNS & THAMES VALLEY (1:200,000)
THE COTSWOLDS (1:110,000)
COTSWOLDS & SEVERN VALLEY (1:200,000)
WALES (1:250,000)
THE SHIRES OF MIDDLE ENGLAND (1:250,000)
THE MID SHIRES (Staffs, Shrops, etc.) (1:200,000)
PEAK DISTRICT (1:100,000)
SNOWDONIA (1:125,000)
YORKSHIRE (1:200,000)
YORKSHIRE DALES (1:125,000)
NORTH YORKSHIRE MOORS (1:125,000)
NORTH WEST ENGLAND (1:200,000)
ISLE OF MAN (1:60,000)
NORTH PENNINES & LAKES (1:200,000)
LAKE DISTRICT (1:75,000)
BORDERS OF ENGLAND & SCOTLAND (1:200,000)
BURNS COUNTRY (1:200,000)
HEART OF SCOTLAND (1:200,000)
GREATER GLASGOW (1:150,000)
EDINBURGH & THE LOTHIANS (1:150,000)
ISLE OF ARRAN (1:63,360)
FIFE (1:100,000)
LOCH LOMOND & TROSSACHS (1:150,000)
ARGYLL THE ISLES & LOCH LOMOND (1:275,000)
PERTHSHIRE, DUNDEE & ANGUS (1:150,000)
FORT WILLIAM, BEN NEVIS, GLEN COE (1:185,000)
IONA (1:10,000) & MULL (1:115,000)
GRAMPIAN HIGHLANDS (1:185,000)
LOCH NESS & INVERNESS (1:150,000)
SKYE & LOCHALSH (1:130,000)
ARGYLL & THE ISLES (1:200,000)
CAITHNESS & SUTHERLAND (1:185,000)
HIGHLANDS OF SCOTLAND (1:275,000)
WESTERN ISLES (1:125,000)
ORKNEY & SHETLAND (1:128,000)
ENGLAND & WALES (1:650,000)
SCOTLAND (1:500,000)
HISTORIC SCOTLAND (1:500,000)
SCOTLAND CLAN MAP (1:625,000)
BRITISH ISLES (1:1,100,000)
GREAT BRITAIN (1:1,100,000)

EUROPEAN LEISURE MAPS

EUROPE (1:3,100,000)
BENELUX (1:600,000)
FRANCE (1:1,000,000)
GERMANY (1:1,000,000)
IRELAND (1:625,000)
ITALY (1:1,000,000)
SPAIN & PORTUGAL (1:1,000,000)
CROSS CHANNEL VISITORS' MAP (1:530,000)
WORLD (1:35,000,000)
WORLD FLAT

TOWNS IN NORTHERN FRANCE STREET ATLAS
BOULOGNE SHOPPERS MAP
CALAIS SHOPPERS MAP
DIEPPE SHOPPERS MAP

ESTATE PUBLICATIONS are also
Distributors in the UK for:

HALLWAG, Switzerland
HEMA, Australia
INTERNATIONAL TRAVEL MAPS, Canada
ORDNANCE SURVEY

Catalogue and prices from:
ESTATE PUBLICATIONS
Bridewell House, Tenterden, Kent. TN30 6EP.
Tel: 01580 764225   Fax: 01580 763720
www.estate-publications.co.uk